Wild & Wacky

ANIMAL CARTOONS FOR KIDS

JONNY HAWKINS

HARVEST HOUSE PUBLISHERS

EUGENE, OREGON

Cover by Terry Dugan Design, Minneapolis, Minnesota

Dedicated to my wild and wacky boys:
Nathaniel and Zachary

WILD & WACKY ANIMAL CARTOONS FOR KIDS
Copyright © 2004 by Jonny Hawkins
Published by Harvest House Publishers
Eugene, Oregon 97402

ISBN 0-7369-1339-4

Printed in the United States of America

04 05 06 07 08 09 10 / BC-MS / 10 9 8 7 6 5 4 3 2 1

BIRDWATCHERS SOCIETY

JONNY HAWKINS

7

9

"He's the ring bear."

Where Canadian Bacon
Comes From

"Well how 'bout that!
Grade A!"

16

"How strong is your
search engine?"

"So far I can only pull a
dust bunny out of it."

19

"Gesundheit."

"You're eating a *worm?* Your mom
is going to have a *fit!*"

23

"I got caught in a
sting operation."

"Excuse the expression, Smokey,
but let's go for the burn."

"I never should have let those
woodpeckers stay with me."

"Bad kitty."

"How about a quick game
of hairball?"

"I remember when he was wise.
Now he's just a smart aleck."

36

"We have ways of making
you quack!"

"Move in front of me.
I want to see what I'd look like
with a hairy chest."

JONNY
HAWKINS

"You have toad rage."

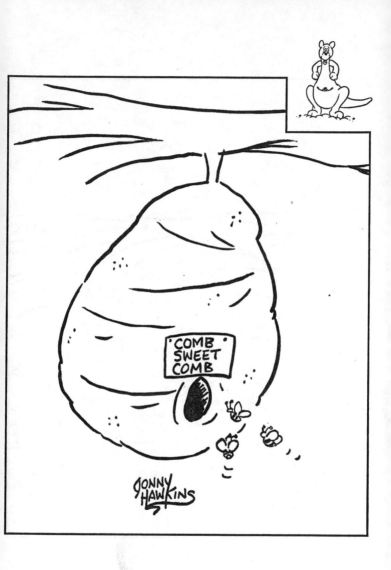

49

"I ordered *antchovies*."

"Yo! I'd like some
cappuccino here!"

Giraffiti

"Yesterday I laughed so hard I
shot a milk snake through my nose."

"What?! You've never seen
a fire ant before?"

Chicken à la king

"Here, let *me* toss the salad.
I was made for it."

"I love the new easy-open
zip lock feature!"

"Try it in a six."

"I've learned to turn
the udder cheek."

"I just had a hot meal.
I touched my jaw to the
electric fence."

"Now I've seen it all:
a bull with a goatee, and
a goat with a nose ring!"

"You've got measles."

"Wooh, that's weird!
Some nectar went down
the wrong pipe!"

Worm Wrestling

"Do you want to go
skin diving?"

"I prefer Easy
Listening music."

68

SHOES

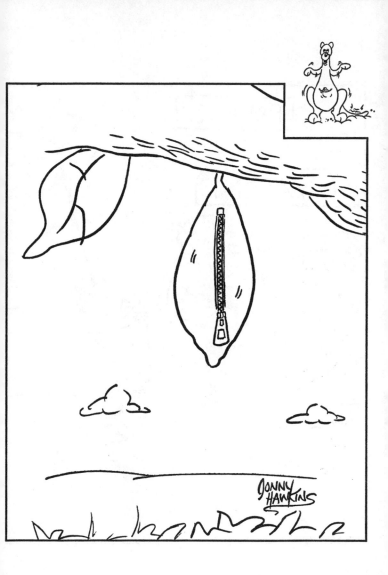

JONNY
HAWKINS

COTTONTAIL CANDY

"I've heard it's
really cheesy!"

"I'm a pointer and I realize
it's not polite to point."

"You drank the waterbed!"

"You're lucky. Everything I eat
goes to my hips."

"Bills, bills, bills."

"That caffeine kept me up
all winter."

"This hippo-pool was
a great idea."

"How do you manage to
keep yourself wrinkled
so beautifully?"

"Uh oh. Now he's
getting serious."

Odor! Odor! Odor in
the court!"

"Murray believes in
a well-balanced diet."

"I didn't *think* your eye was
that black before."

"For your insomnia, I'm going to
prescribe sleepy seeds."

The Fangaroo

"Man, that was a great tree!
Care for a toothpick?"

"Junior won't come out...
he's watching T.V. All he ever is
anymore is a pouch potato!"

Hyperpotamus

"We're showing a movie tonight.
Would you mind
filling this with popcorn?"

"I have a taste for skunks...which
is how I got the nickname
'Odor Eater'."

"Oh, pay no mind to Harold...
he's moping because I just had
him re-upholstered."

"Nice talking to you, but I've
gotta go play the organ...
it's back to the grind!"

When Whales Play

"I see you bought some
beachfront property."

"Is that *your* banana
or *mine*?"

"I'll take the
Nutcracker Suite."

"Hang around the *jaguars*, son,
because *cheetahs*
never prosper."

"The little one? Oh,
he's at Cub Scouts."

"Hey...my ride is down!
Can I get a jump start?"

"Look, I don't mind your zebra
stories...but cut to the chase!"

"Another charlie horse?"

"Oh, I just love
a little horse play..."

"Are you genuine leather?"

"When did you get the
new microwave?"

"I'm in home school."

"I am not a big fan of the
new cubicles."

"Careful! I hear it has a Net."

"I can't decide if I like your
new choker or not."

"Grounded again?"

POOL SHARK

"Her eyes are like mine,
but she definitely has
your trunk."

136

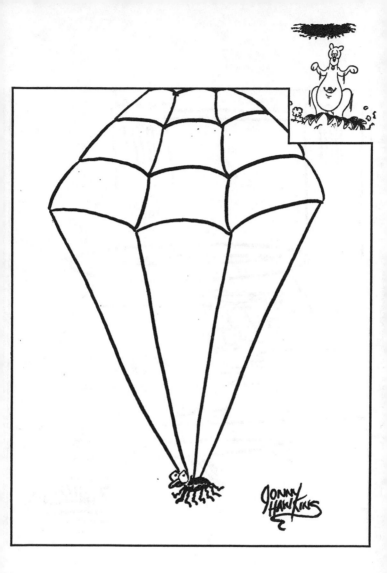

143

"I thought we agreed
he shouldn't be eating
table scraps."

"Cool. *Now* let's try it
with bubblewrap."

"He can come out and
play when he's done eating
his homework."

A Detroit tiger

Embarrassing monkey moments

"...I just ate a rancid moose.
Ya gotta mint?"

"I just invented
online skating."

"I'll pay you five bucks to crawl
inside my shell and scratch a
40-year-old itch on my back."

"Whoowee!...Somebody around here
has swampfoot!"

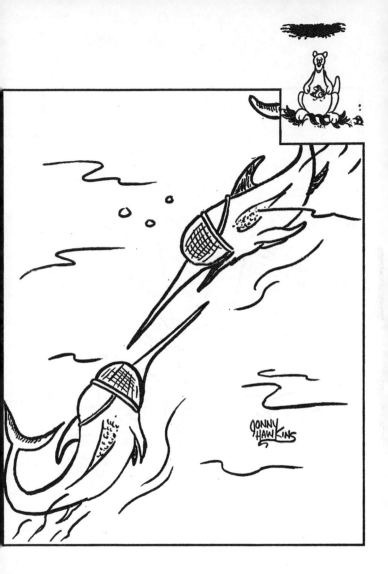

YAK-IN-THE-BOX

Karate Kid meets Lamb Chop

"Oh, nothing...just trying
to stay in sheep shape."

"Got any mud pies?"

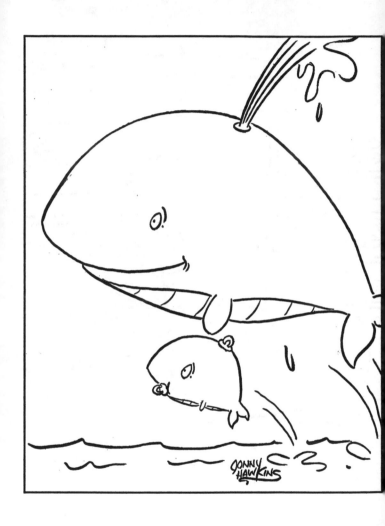

170

"It's a new whistle
for ducks...it features
'call wading'."

"Billy! I didn't know you ran a
food delivery service!"

"I made a decision that if I was going
to spend my life digging underground,
I was going to wear safety goggles."